Guns at School

A Systems Thinking Perspective

by Barry Richmond

created with

STELLA™ software

www.iseesystems.com
Phone 603 448 4990   Fax 603 448 4992
Technical Support: support@iseesystems.com

Contents

Preface

By Katherine Richmond
Hanover, New Hampshire

Barry Richmond began studying and teaching System Dynamics in the late 1970s while a graduate student at MIT. His work in that field led to an interest in Systems Thinking. Experimentation with this exciting new approach to thinking led to a missionary zeal to build bridges to the mainstream.

Barry's passion for making Systems Thinking accessible to anyone studying any issue broke the mold. Rather than reserving Systems Thinking for ivory tower pursuits, he saw it being used in elementary school classrooms to teach story plotlines, in businesses to understand manufacturing processes, or by medical researchers to investigate cancer. Applying Systems Thinking to pressing social problems was Barry's special interest.

His colleague, Steve Peterson, remembers:

"Barry often talked about the value of a Systems Thinking framework as a vehicle for "building a better argument" about the causes and potential solutions to pressing problems facing society. Barry's view was that it "ought to be possible" to use simple systems diagrams and simulations to help people develop a richer picture of what's going on out there in the world so that they might then act on that understanding."

In his book *An Introduction to Systems Thinking with STELLA*®, written for use with the leading edge Systems Thinking software tool he developed, Barry wrote:

"Why do we continue to make so little progress in addressing our many, very pressing social concerns? My answer is that the way we think, communicate, and learn is outdated. As a result, the way we act creates problems. And then, we're ill equipped to address them because of the way we've been taught to think, communicate, and learn. However, it is the premise of Systems Thinking that it is possible to evolve our thinking, communicating, and learning capacities. As we do, we will be able to make progress in addressing the compelling slate of issues that challenge our viability."

Barry was always looking for new ways to teach Systems Thinking, to make it accessible, and to make it applicable. In 2001, he began writing Stories of the Month. These stories were designed to show how STELLA, the Systems Thinking software tool he developed, could map and then model a thought process. More importantly, the stories were designed to stimulate discussion of pressing issues, to drive towards a shared understanding of problems, causes, and the best possible solutions.

Systems Thinking is a *disciplined* way of understanding the *dynamic relationships* between things so that you can make better choices and avoid *unintended consequences.*

Each Story of the Month dealt with a very real, well-documented social issue. All stories are as topical today as they were when Barry wrote them. Story of the Month titles included:

• *Can Energy Prices be Passed on to the Consumer?*
• *Deficits/Surpluses, Tax Cuts and Social Security Promises: Lifting the Fog*
• *A Systems Thinking Look at Terrorism*
• *The Dynamics of Fear*
• *Enron — Partnerships and "Partnerships"*
• *The Israeli-Palestinian Conflict*
• *Reforming School Reform*

and

• *Guns at School.*

The use of guns by students at all grade levels remains a haunting problem. Like most social problems, it is one with many complicated, related causes, and many complicated, possible solutions. Those relationships and solutions make it a great candidate for Systems Thinking.

Guns at School first appeared in 2001. Every attempt has been made to update background statistics and information. The Systems Thinking concepts and models remain relevant and unchanged.

Katherine and Barry Richmond shared their lives for 33 years. Together they raised a family and promoted Systems Thinking through development of the intuitive software tools, STELLA® and iThink®. Katherine was a member of the original STELLA development team.

CHAPTER 1
Applying Systems Thinking

The Problem of Guns at School

One of the most frightening trends to appear over the last decade has been the rise of gun-related violence at schools. Between 1994 and 1999, there were 220 school associated violent events resulting in 253 deaths. Of those deaths, 188 were caused by firearms that had been brought to school (National Education Association, Health Information Network). Countless other children have been physically injured or emotionally traumatized by in-school gun violence. In 1998, the National Education Association reported that nearly 8% of adolescents in urban junior and senior high schools miss school because they are afraid to go.

A myriad of reasons have been cited for the emergence of this chilling phenomenon. These include: escalating levels of violence in video games, television and movies; media coverage; declining parental involvement; erosion of moral standards and values; the widespread availability of guns; and rising levels of student alienation and rage.

In May 2001, a *USA Today* article, "Rage, not guns, blamed for school violence," quoted statements made by Rod Paige, then US Secretary of Education, on CBS' Face the Nation. The article pointed to shootings in California and Pennsylvania that had left two students dead and 13 people wounded. Secretary Paige said,

> *"Students' alienation and rage is the biggest factor in school shootings. Addressing that problem, rather than changing the gun laws, should be the priority. …guns cannot take blame because there have been reports of students plotting violence with bombs and other devices. We need to look at the cause of the situation."*

If guns *aren't* responsible, then what is? How do we begin to think about the problem? How do we find solutions? Until we have a solid grip on the relationships responsible for producing and maintaining the scary phenomenon of school students shooting their peers and teachers, we have scant hope of doing much to effectively address it.

A progression of factors has been cited as a cause of gun violence at school. They are:
• students humiliating peers
• humiliation leading to rage and alienation
• rage needing an outlet
• access to guns
• media coverage leading to "copy cat" events

Since school gun violence is a complex problem involving several, interrelated factors that change over time, it is an issue that can be explored using Systems Thinking.

What is Systems Thinking?

One definition of Systems Thinking is…

> a **disciplined** way of understanding the **dynamic relationships** between things so that you can make better choices and avoid **unintended consequences**.

Let's examine the important components of that definition.

The **discipline** of Systems Thinking is to examine the overall cause of a problem by taking time to note the relationships between factors. For example, to understand guns at school we have to consider how behaviors lead to emotions, how emotions build, how violence provides outlet for emotions, how outcomes might inspire future events. That's much more illuminating, less overwhelming, and probably more complete, than looking at the entire complexity of a problem all at once.

When we start thinking about a problem, we create a mental model, an idea of what instigates trouble and what corrective actions might be taken. Systems Thinkers explore those mental models by writing them down. They create visual models either by drawing them or using a software program. Either method works — though software provides greater flexibility and less erasing! STELLA® was created by Barry Richmond to make Systems Thinking and models easier to document and share.

Models reveal the story of a problem. They show how it starts and how behaviors lead to events. Most importantly, they help us test ideas for how outcomes, especially bad outcomes, can be changed.

Indicating change is a very important part of Systems Thinking. Systems Thinking models describe **dynamic relationships**; they show how systems operate over time and how conditions within those systems change. For example, a model of school violence might illustrate a series of humiliating events that build rage in the humiliated student. That's an important change in the system and it happens through a series of events that occur over the course of weeks or months.

Avoiding unintended consequences is one benefit of thinking systemically. Consider this example. Our mental model assumes that school shootings are simply the result of kids mimicking video games and television violence, so we ban video games and television. But suppose banning media exposure caused other, unintended consequences like an increase in the student drop-out rate or a decrease in student participation in community service projects promoted by the media. Systems Thinking gives you a framework for exploring the impacts and ripple effects of an action or change. It provides a structure for communication and discussion of the issues.

In the next chapter we'll define key Systems Thinking concepts that, together, provide the foundation for a disciplined approach to problem solving. Once we understand those concepts, we'll apply them to the problem of guns at school. We'll present a model of the problem showing the related causes. And then, we'll search for high leverage points, the best possible solutions to school gun violence.

While Systems Thinking does not require software, we will apply Systems Thinking concepts to school gun violence using a model created with STELLA. The CD that accompanies this book includes the model and documentation.

CHAPTER 2

Systems Thinking: A Quick Primer

Laundry Lists versus Systems Thinking

As we noted in Chapter 1, Systems Thinking gives us a disciplined approach to exploring a problem and potential solutions. We can best appreciate Systems Thinking if we consider how it compares to another widely used thought process – laundry list thinking.

Laundry list thinking, also called critical success factors thinking, involves list making. It typically involves answering the question: "What are all the factors that influence this outcome?" After a school shooting, we might generate a laundry list of factors that looks like this:

Factors leading to shootings in school

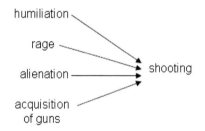

This list has several useful characteristics. It's simple. It's easy to read. And as far as it goes, it is a good start at thinking about the factors that lead to shootings. Unfortunately, lists such as these have some serious shortcomings. Among them:

• They assume the factors leading to an outcome go in one direction. The factor leads to an outcome, but there's no potential for the outcome to feed back to influence the factor. For example, a school shooting outcome would likely have an impact on factors such as rage and alienation.

• They assume that the factors are independent of one another, missing, for example, the interdependencies between things such as alienation and anger.

• They lead to a static view of the problem and its potential solutions, "if we could just make access to guns go away, the problem would be fixed."

Systems Thinking goes beyond list making to the creation of diagrams that show how the system operates (operational view) and the relationships between the different system parts (closed-loop view). Systems Thinkers don't ask, "What are all the factors that influence gun-related school violence?" Rather, they want to develop an operational specification of what causes it — a single, multi-faceted theory that can be used to test solutions. Again, using our guns at school example, Systems Thinking might generate this:

Some students are relentlessly humiliated by their peers at school. This humiliation leads to rage and alienation. Rage requires outlet. Alienation allows the student to disassociate from or feel superior to his peers. When guns are accessible, brought to school and shot at peers, they provide an outlet to the rage.

This type of thinking leads to the following diagram, where the impact of the outcome and the interdependencies between factors create a dynamic view of the situation.

Interdependent, closed-loop view of shootings in school

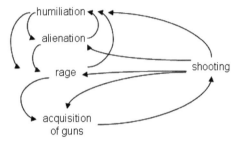

Systems Thinking and System Dynamics give us tools and concepts to use when making operational models. STELLA, the software we'll be using to explore the guns at school model, represents these concepts with icons. Used together, they tell a story.

The STELLA icons are operational in nature. They tell a story "like it is" and enable you to see events and outcomes with your mind's eye, and your real eyes. Ambiguities and chances for miscommunication are greatly reduced.

The Language of STELLA

When we tell or write a story we use language that follows rules of grammar. Nouns define people, places, and things. Verbs relate actions, and so on. Systems Thinking models built using STELLA also have a language that follows rules of grammar and can be connected to tell a story.

The two most important elements of the STELLA language are the stock and the flow. Stocks are nouns and represent accumulations of things: students, guns, or schools, and states of being: humiliation, rage, and alienation. Students collect guns. Rage builds.

Stocks are represented by a rectangle. In the Guns at School model, one stock is "Available Guns." Another grisly stock is "Cumulative Deaths in School from Guns."

Available   Cumulative Deaths in
Guns   School from Guns

Flows are verbs in STELLA. They represent actions or activities that fill or drain stocks. Like stocks, flows can be physical or non-physical in nature. Physical flows are obtaining guns (builds stock of guns) or killing people (builds stock of casualties). Non-physical flows are teasing (builds stock of humiliation) or increasing feelings of rage.

Flows are represented by directed pipes, with valves attached. In the Guns at School model, one flow represents the action of "people being killed at school by guns."

people being
killed at school
by guns

Stocks and flows are simple, but extremely powerful. They characterize how things work in reality. They accumulate and they flow. Any dynamic system can be represented using stocks and flows.

When we join a flow with a stock, we begin to tell a story. "People being killed at school by guns" causes the "Cumulative Deaths in School from Guns" to increase.

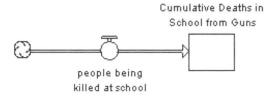

Cumulative Deaths in
School from Guns

people being
killed at school

This is a good time to point out that there are numbers, and sometimes equations, associated with these icons in STELLA models. A particular student might have access to 10 guns in his family's gun closet. His stock of guns would be 10. If that student shoots 15 students, the number of people killed would increase by 15.

It takes more than nouns and verbs to tell a complete story. Connectors and converters are other important elements of the STELLA language.

Connectors serve as conjunctions in that they join the various components of a model. Connectors transmit actions and information required to generate flows. In the guns at school model, one connector joins "Level of Rage" to "becoming enraged." Connectors are represented by an arrow.

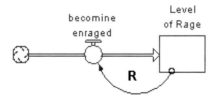

becoming
enraged

Level
of Rage

R

When a connector links a stock back to its flow, a **feedback loop** is created. In Guns at School, we'll see a reinforcing feedback loop where students are unable to vent their rage. That leads to more rage. If acts of humiliation continue, the stock of rage will spiral out of control. The stock of rage feeds back to affect the "becoming enraged" flow.

Reinforcing feedback loops operate as "vicious (or virtuous!) cycles." Vicious cycles feed upon themselves and are compounding in nature. Push on something that's controlled by a reinforcing feedback loop, and you'll start an avalanche!

Counteracting or balancing feedback loops are just the opposite. They resist change and work to maintain stability. If you push on something that's being controlled by a counteracting feedback loop, you'll experience "push back" in the opposite direction.

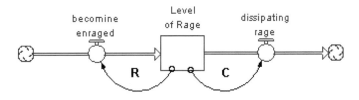

You can imagine a counteracting feedback loop between the stock of rage and the flow of dissipating rage. The rate of dissipation depends on the amount of stocked rage. The feedback loop between the Level of Rage and dissipating rage keeps rage from spiraling out of control.

Feedback loops control growth and stability in natural, physical, and social systems. That's what makes them a critical concept in System Thinking.

The primary role of **converters** is to function as adverbs. They modify flows and tell how quickly or slowly an action happens. In the Guns at School model, one converter represents the "average # of people killed per shooting incident per year." Converters are represented by circles.

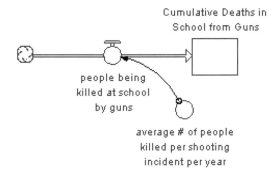

Real understanding of these tools and concepts comes through application. In the next chapter, STELLA's stocks, flows, connectors and converters will be used to create a visual model of school gun violence. You may want to refer back to this chapter if you need a quick review of definitions.

CHAPTER 3
Understanding the System

In this chapter, we'll walk through a model that was created with STELLA to examine the problem of Guns at School. The model serves several purposes:

1. It helps us understand how to apply Systems Thinking to a complicated social issue.

2. It gets us thinking and talking about the problem of guns at school.

3. It helps us discover high leverage points or the best possible solutions.

Before we dig into the problem itself, we'll walk through the model and make sure we understand its components. First we'll unfurl the physical aspects of gun acquisition and shootings. Then we'll step through the psychological components of alienation and rage dynamics. This is a model for a single school. Events in the model occur over a 40-week school year. The stocks of rage, alienation, students with guns, etc. are averages for the entire student population.

You may want to follow these pages (and/or chapters 4 and 5) using the STELLA Guns at School model included on your CD.

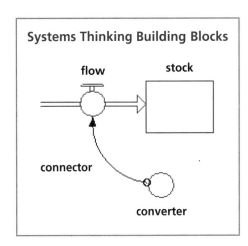

Systems Thinking Building Blocks

flow   stock

connector

converter

Unfurl the Structure of the System

The focal point of the story is people (mostly, but not only, students) being killed or injured at school by gun violence. In the language of Systems Thinking, the act of being killed, injured, or traumatized is represented as a "flow."

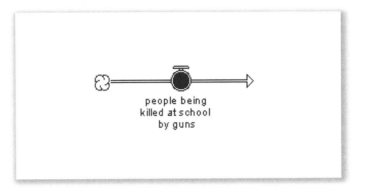

Flows (i.e., actions) leave "traces" – which is to say, "accumulations." Accumulations in the language of Systems Thinking are called "stocks." Stocks are represented by rectangles. This stock captures the cumulative number of people who are killed by the act of gun violence.

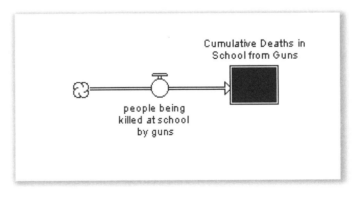

Should a shooting occur in this model, the number of "people being killed at school by guns" will be based on the average number of people who have been killed per shooting incident over the last five years. Long term averages are used instead of data from individual events to show overall behavior over a period of time.

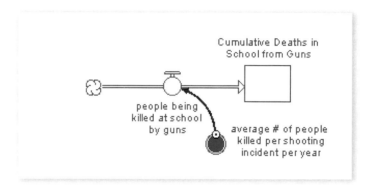

The "trigger" for the act of violence is the number of students who have (or have immediate access to) guns. That number is a stock that builds up as the average level of rage within the student body mounts, and kids consider giving voice to their anger by violent means.

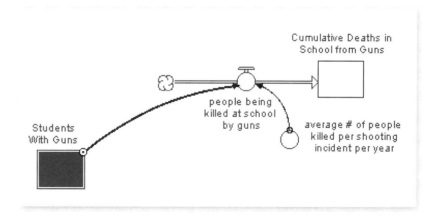

The population of students with guns is fed by an arming flow.

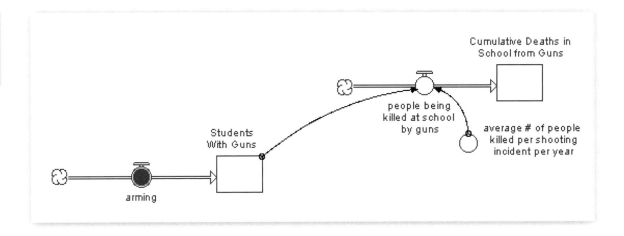

In order to become armed, students must secure a gun. In order to secure a gun, there must be a stock of guns that are available to be secured by students.

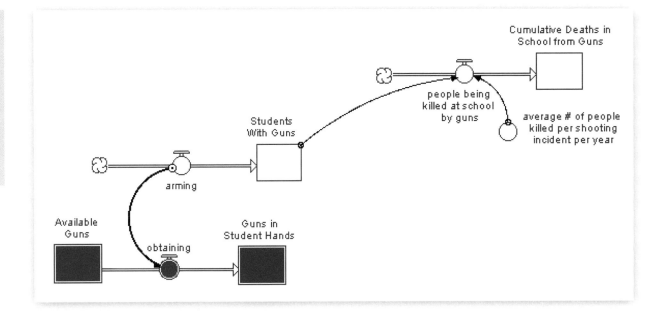

The number of students who arm themselves is assumed to adjust to an "indicated number."

An indicated number is an expected number due to other factors. "Indicated students with guns" is the number of students expected to arm themselves due to other factors.

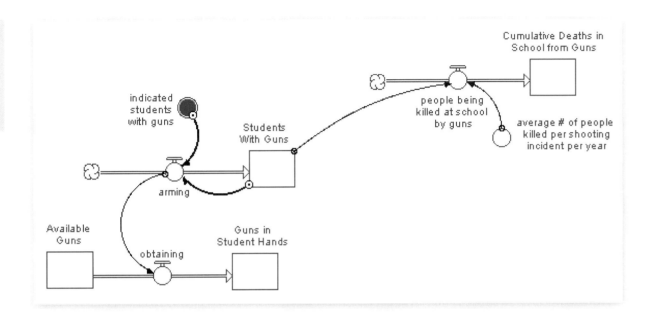

That "indicated number" is determined by how enraged the student population is feeling and the number of students that desire to arm themselves. It provides the link from the psychological to the physical structure of the model.

Here we see that the "indicated students from rage" converter is special. It is defined by a graphical function that shows the relationship between the level of rage and number of enraged students. We'll talk more about these graphical functions in Chapter 5.

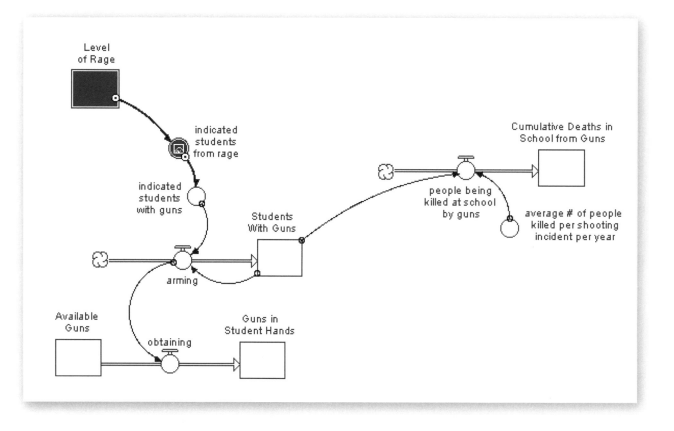

The "indicated number" of students who will seek to obtain guns is assumed to be impacted by media coverage. The model assumes that the media (TV, movies, etc.) inadvertently encourages students to arm themselves – the so-called "copycat" effect.

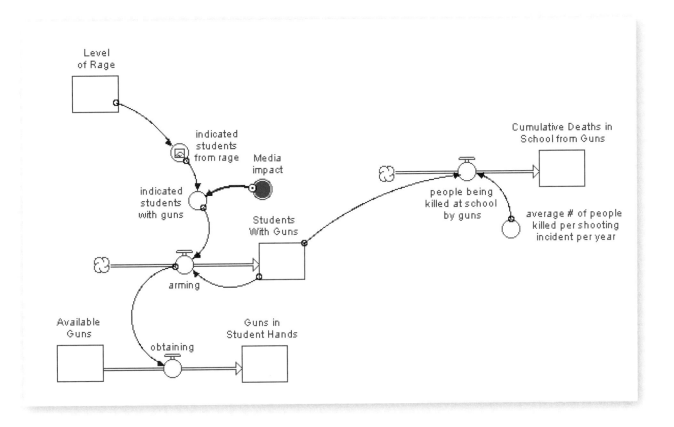

Even if students want to give voice to their rage by seeking retribution with guns, the lack of access to firearms can stymie those desires. The model assumes that the availability of guns influences...

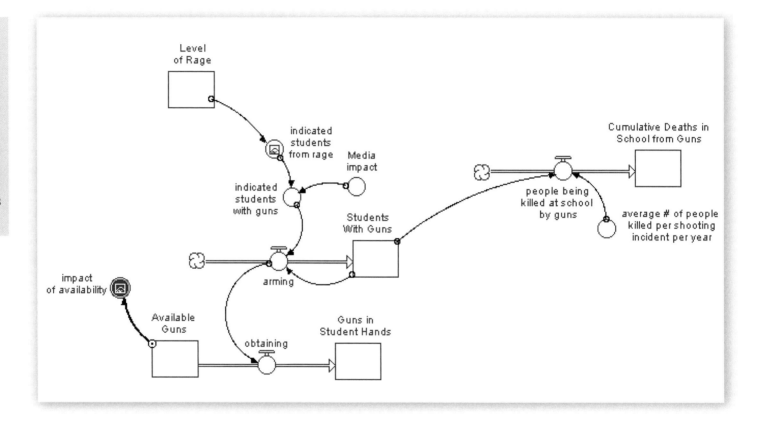

...how long it takes for students to acquire a gun if they are seeking to do that. The higher the availability of guns, the shorter the delay in obtaining them.

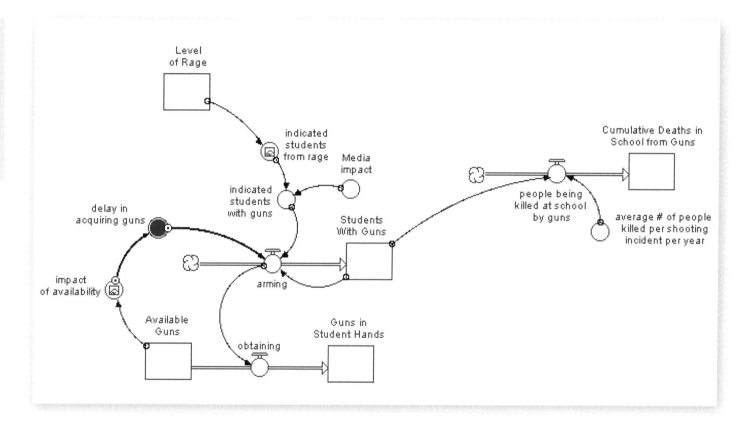

Rage, the fundamental driver of the arming activity, like any stock or accumulation, builds up for one reason: its inflow exceeds its outflow. The model assumes the inflow is driven by...

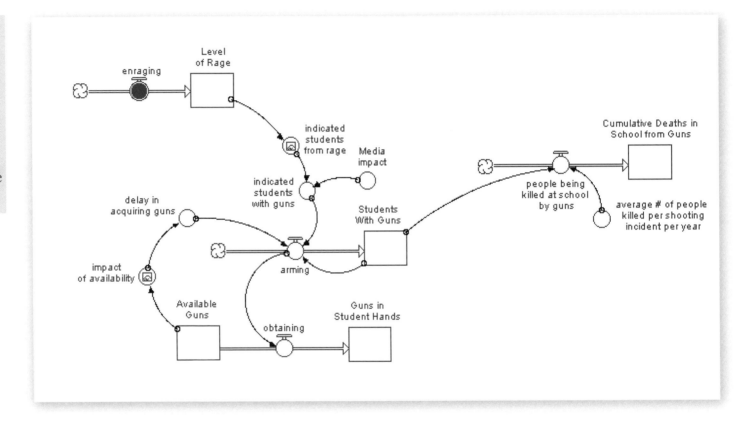

...a flow of humiliating activities. In virtually every recorded incident of gun violence at school, the perpetrator(s) experienced (or perceived that they experienced) some humiliation at the hands of one or more classmates. Humiliating acts are enraging! But there is more to the story.

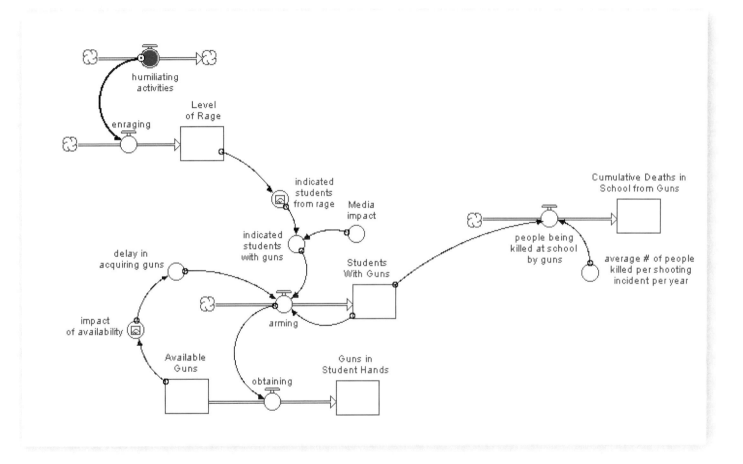

The amount of rage inspired by each act of humiliation is not assumed to be constant! Instead, the more enraged the student is, at the time the humiliating act is committed, the bigger the contribution to rage the act inspires!

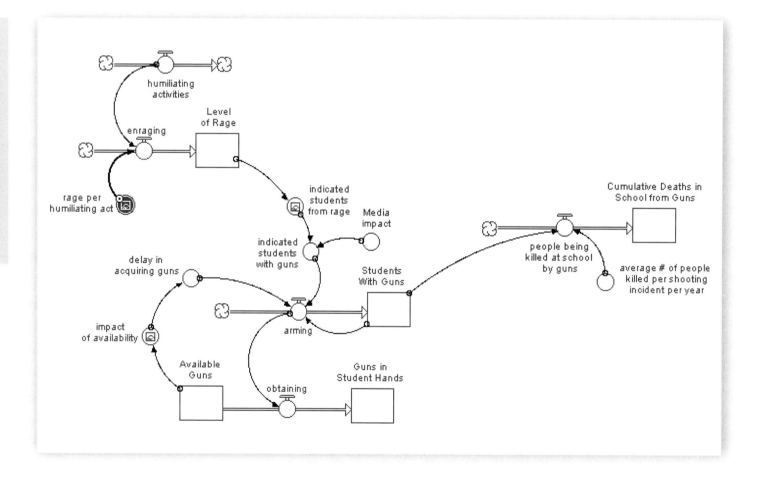

This all leads to a reinforcing feedback loop **(R)**. In this case, the loop operates as a vicious cycle.

In cases where students are unable to dissipate their rage and no one intervenes or helps, additional acts of humiliation will cause the stock of rage to spiral out of control. One option for venting overwhelming rage is violent reaction.

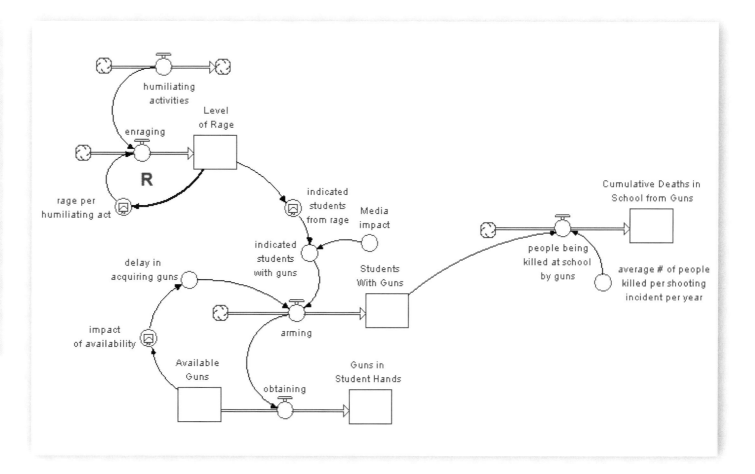

But venting — or dissipating rage — does not have to include violence. There are other, more productive, ways to control the outflow of rage. If the outflow can be kept wide open, students who become enraged will be able to control their anger by dissipating it in non-violent ways— before it reaches overwhelming levels.

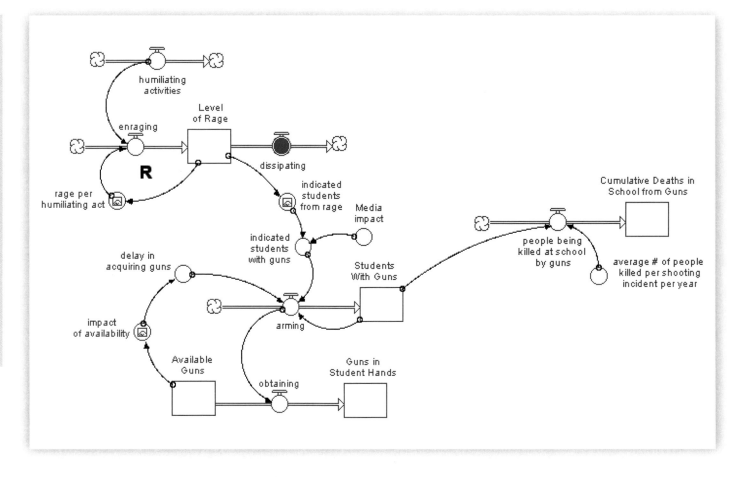

The rate at which students are able to vent their rage is not assumed to be a constant.

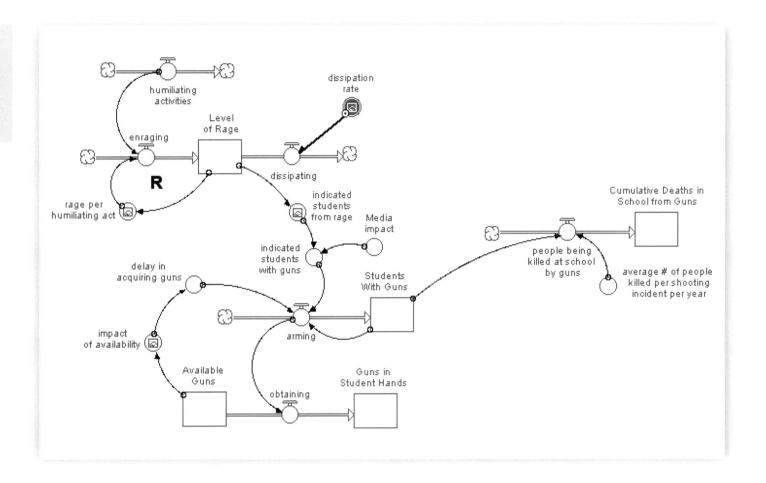

Instead, it's assumed to depend on how alienated the student(s) is feeling. It is assumed that the more alienated from classmates the student feels, the more difficulty they will have in dissipating their rage. In effect, one important operational role that friends, and a social network in general, play is to help the student to deal with the anger that results from being subjected to humiliation.

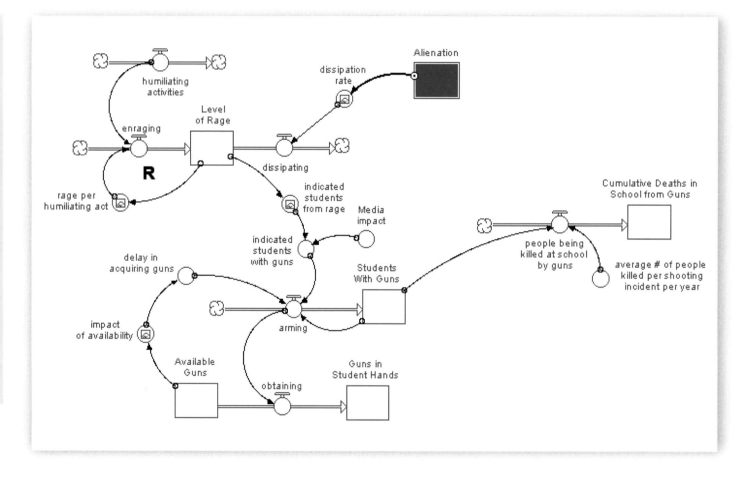

And the plot thickens. It is assumed that humiliating activities drive the buildup of feelings of alienation. That is, when one is humiliated, they feel isolated and alone — as if the "whole world" is singling them out for abuse.

And so, humiliation generates a "double whammy" on rage. Humiliating acts directly drive up the inflow of rage. But they also intensify the humiliated person's sense of alienation. Increased alienation then shuts down the outflow from rage, causing rage to climb even higher than it otherwise would. Nasty!

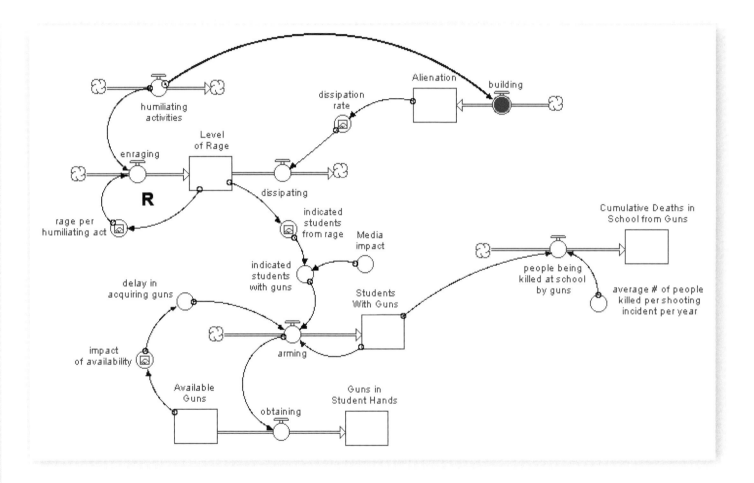

Each act of humiliation builds a certain amount of alienation. And that amount is not constant!

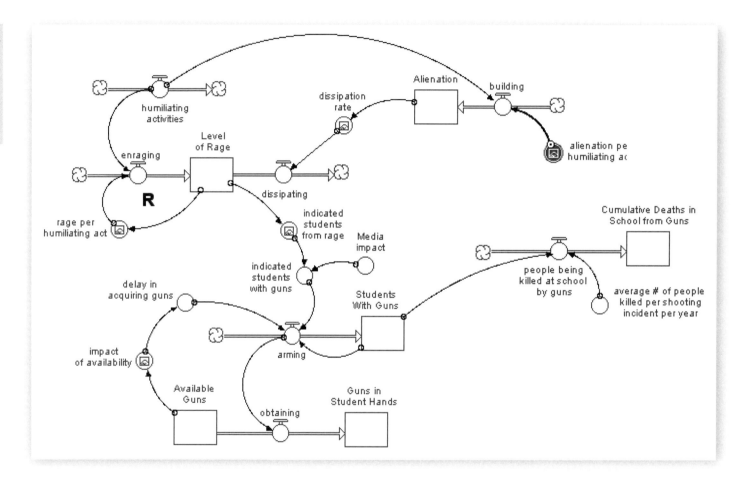

It is assumed that as alienation increases, the amount of alienation that is generated per humiliating act also increases. This is another vicious cycle — hence the "R."

Alienation is assumed to drain at some rate — which, as you will see, can be influenced by various initiatives.

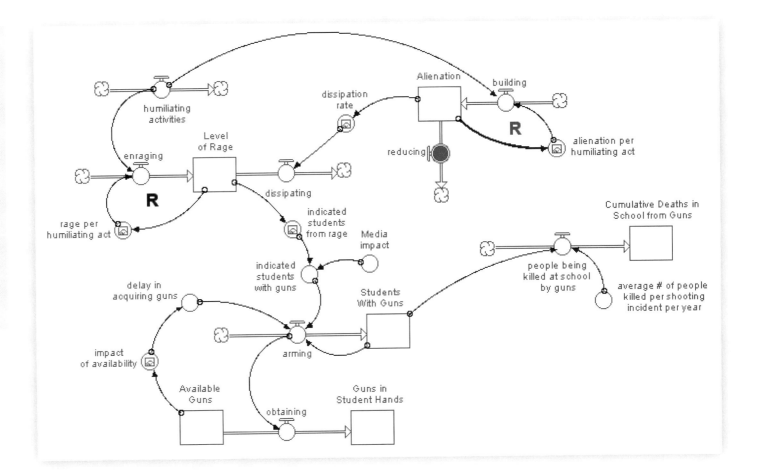

This concludes the cook's tour of the basic structure of the model. Later on, you'll have the opportunity to see how a variety of initiatives designed to reduce gun violence "fit into" the structure.

Take a final look at the major aspects of the system. The physical aspects of gun acquisition and shootings (bottom half of model) are linked by the stock of "Students with Guns." Remember this is the "trigger" for acts of violence.

The psychological aspects of the model include two reinforcing feedback loops that drive the buildup of alienation and rage. (top half of model). Note that rage and alienation are connected by "dissipation rate." It is assumed that the more alienated from classmates the student feels, the more difficulty they will have dissipating their rage.

Finally, the psychological aspects and the physical aspects of the model are linked by "indicated students from rage" — the key to whether or not enraged students arm themselves.

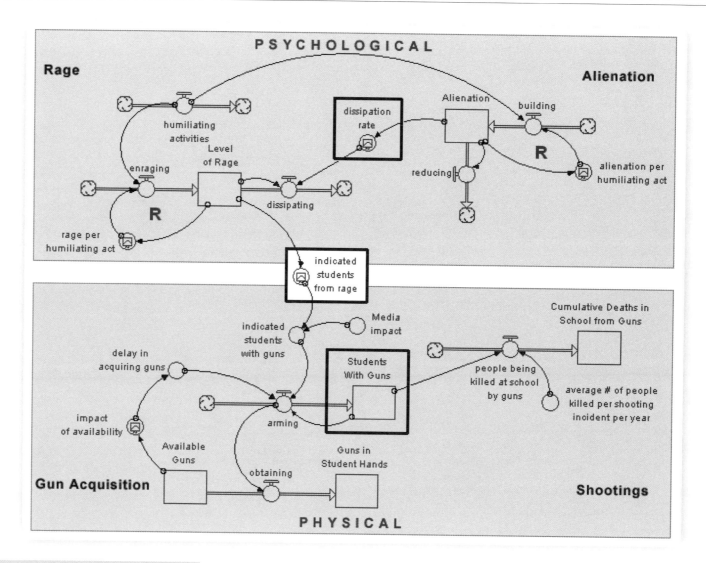

CHAPTER 4

A Progression of Interesting Experiments

One of the reasons it is so difficult to "learn from experience" in the social arena is that it's impossible to do "controlled experiments" in the real world. When scientists conduct laboratory experiments, they take great pains to ensure that they change only one thing at a time and "hold all else constant." That is what enables scientists to draw conclusions about "what is causing what" in their experiment.

"Holding all else constant" in a social system is *impossible* — not just in practice, but in *principle*! That's because social systems are "alive" and "unbounded" by laboratory walls. As is well known, just observing systems, *changes* them! That's why computer simulation can be such a valuable tool for those seeking to make progress in understanding important social issues — like gun violence in schools.

This section provides a simple laboratory for experimenting with a variety of policy initiatives that address the school gun violence issue. You will be guided through a progression of experiments that test each initiative, in *isolation*, to see its impact on gun-related violence. Each experiment involves running a computer simulation of the model. The results are displayed on a behavior over time graph.

The progression of experiments is tightly choreographed to introduce initiatives one-at-a-time in order to build your understanding in a systematic manner. As is traditional in a "systems" policy analysis, we'll begin by looking at a base case — the model with no initiatives applied. After studying the base case, we'll run though the experiments in a "free lunch" manner. That is, neither the costs nor the logistics of implementing any of the initiatives is considered. You wave a magic wand, and they're implemented. The idea is to ensure that an initiative is worth pursuing, before investing the time to model the associated implementation costs and logistical considerations.

There are seven experiments that consider initiatives in three categories:

Gun-related Initiatives
1. Screening
2. Disarming
3. Restricting Access

Media Initiatives
4. Anti-copycat Initiative

Student Coping Skills Initiatives
5. Rage Management
6. Alienation Management
7. Humiliation Management

In Chapter 5, you will have the opportunity to experiment with combinations of initiatives, and with varying underlying assumptions in the model, in a completely free-form way.

Note: We recommend you follow the progression of experiments using the CD that accompanies this book. This chapter assumes you are using the software. If you prefer to simply read through the experiments and results, you can skip the instructions for using the software.

Running the Base Case

Before we begin the experiments and implement the initiatives, we'll run a base case. We'll compare the subsequent experiments' results to the base case to understand how initiatives impact school gun violence.

To run the base case using the CD:

1. Select *A Progression of Interesting Experiments* from the Guns at School menu.

2. Click the *To Lab* link at the bottom of the screen. You should now be at *A Policy Laboratory Dashboard*, ready to run the base case.

3. Turn the Interpretation switch "on" by clicking on it.

4. Click the Run button. The simulation will run and the results will be drawn on the graph.

In the base case, the model is set up to represent a school in which there is a healthy stream of humiliating actions being generated, and where at least a few members of the student body have access to guns. In addition, there are no initiatives in place to address the consequent dynamics. As a result, when rage and alienation grow among the population being subjected to the humiliation, a shooting incident occurs. Subsequent simulations, which will have one of the seven initiatives "turned on," should be examined relative to this "no initiative" case.

Note that the x-axis of the results graph represents weeks to show how rage and alienation build over time. The y-axis represents a relative magnitude of rage and alienation to show how much they build. All results graphs represent time on the x-axis and magnitude on the y-axis.

Base Case Results

A Policy Laboratory Dashboard

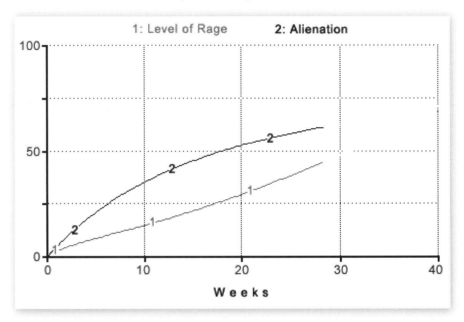

A Simulation-Generated Shooting Has Occurred!

Number of people killed in the incident   **7**

Week Number   **28**

Note: Your simulation results may differ due to a built-in variance for randomness.

Running the Experiments

Each of the seven experiments considers how a particular initiative impacts gun violence. We're looking for positive impacts; initiatives that stop gun violence in our modeled school. We'll experiment with each initiative by running a simulation. Results, or the impact of the initiative, will be shown on a graph. You will either hear a shooting, or not.

You'll run each experiment the same way following the steps outlined below. These steps are not repeated for each experiment so refer back to this page if you need a refresher.

To conduct each experiment:

1. Make sure the Interpretation switch is "on." Turn on by clicking on it.

2. Click the *To initiatives* link so that you are on the *Policy Initiatives* screen.

3. Set the dial of the Knob Device for the initiative you are looking at to 100. To do this, click on the knob and drag it around to 100.

4. Click on *Back* to return to the Policy Laboratory Dashboard.

5. Click on the *Run* button (at the top left of the screen) to run the simulation.

After each simulation, you will receive some descriptive information that will help you to assess why the initiative generated the result it did. Click *Back* and then *To Initiatives* after the simulation in order to review the logic of the initiative (directions on that screen will tell you how to do this).

We'll do the first experiment, the Screening Initiative, together.

To run the Screening Initiative:

1. Go to the Policy Initiatives screen and set the Screening Initiative knob to 100. This sets the initiative to 100%, fully implemented.

2. Click the *Back* link to return to the Policy Laboratory Dashboard.

3. Make sure the Interpretation Switch is turned on and click the Run button.

4. Click the *Back* link to return to the Policy Laboratory Dashboard.

5. Then click the *To Initiatives* link to run the next experiment.

Gun-Related Initiatives

1. Screening Initiative

The Screening Initiative aims to ensure that guns do not get into the schools. Measures would include metal detectors at school entrances, random locker inspections, and so forth.

A value of 0 means the initiative is not in place. A value of 100 means the initiative is fully implemented and 100% effective – no guns get into the school building, and no people are killed inside the school with guns.

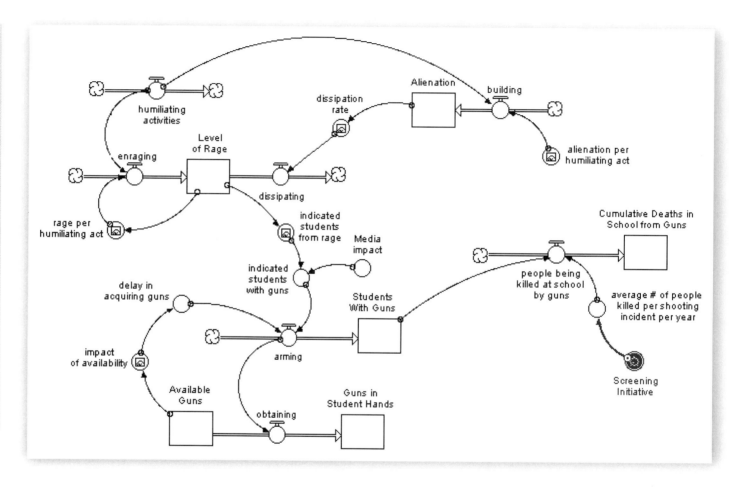

Screening Initiative Results
A Policy Laboratory Dashboard

The Screening Initiative is ineffective in this model. The reason is that preventing guns from getting in the school, or finding them in lockers once they are there, does nothing to address the (model-generated) fundamental cause of shootings in school, which is the build-up of rage. Screening in this context, is "scraping burnt toast" – which is to say, too little, too late.

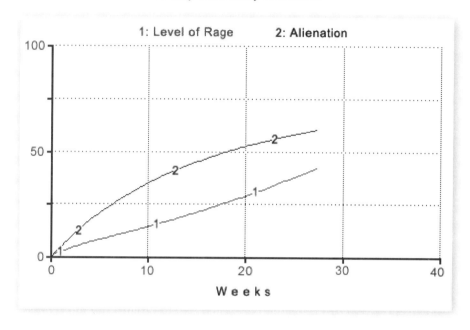

As shown by the results to the right, a screening initiative still resulted in shootings on school grounds — not inside the school building. So, even at 100%, a screening initiative that effectively keeps guns out of the school building would not be 100% effective in eliminating school killings.

As you work through the next experiments remember that a value of 0 means the initiative is not in place. A value of 100 means the initiative is fully implemented and 100% effective at what they were meant to do. (Though, that doesn't mean they are 100% effective in reducing or stopping shootings.) Values between 0 and 100 have corresponding meanings in terms of effectiveness.

Results of implementing the remaining six initiatives will be discussed now. If you need a reminder of the instructions for how to run an experiment, return to page 37 for help.

A Simulation-Generated Shooting Has Occurred!

Number of people killed in the incident	3
Week Number	26

Note: Your simulation results may differ due to a built-in variance for randomness.

Gun-Related Initiatives

2. Disarming Initiative

The Disarming Initiative seeks to get the guns that are in the hands of students, out of their hands! Measures would include intelligence programs to detect students who are harboring guns, and who have ready access to guns.

A value of 0 means no initiative is in effect. A value of 100 means the initiative is 100% effective in detecting and removing guns – though this does not mean that all guns are detected and removed instantly! Intermediate values indicate corresponding levels of initiative effectiveness (i.e., a value of 20% means the initiative is 20% effective, and so forth).

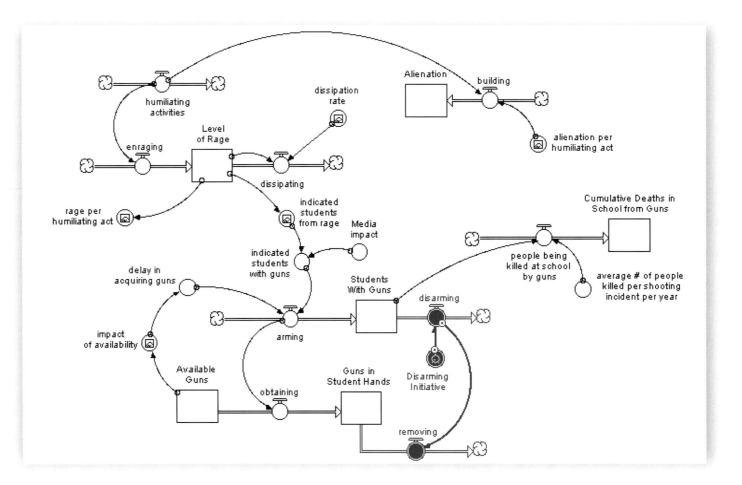

Disarming Initiative Results
A Policy Laboratory Dashboard

Like Screening, the Disarming Initiative is "closing the barn doors after the horses are already out." The initiative in no way addresses the build-up of rage, but rather only seeks to prevent students from having the wherewithal to act on their feelings through gun-related violence. Even an extremely effective Disarming initiative could not possibly catch every kid with a gun, every time. It only takes one kid to slip through the cracks to cause a lot of harm.

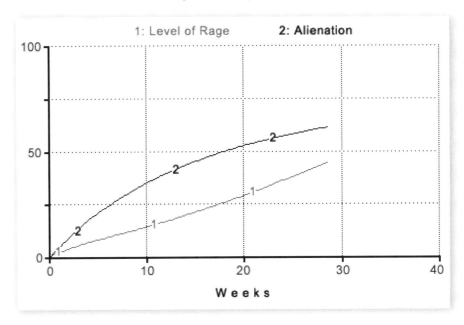

A Simulation-Generated Shooting Has Occurred!

Number of people killed in the incident   7

Week Number   28

Note: Your simulation results may differ due to a built-in variance for randomness.

Gun-Related Initiatives

3. Restricting Access Initiative

This initiative is two-pronged. First, the availability of guns is reduced by restricting access to guns that are "already out there." Measures could include stiff penalties for parents/adults who enable kids to gain access to their guns.

The second prong of the initiative is to slow the increase in the guns becoming available. Tougher licensing requirements could be one approach.

If access to guns by students is reduced, it will stifle students' ability to translate their rage into gun-related violence. The model assumes that availability impacts the amount of time it takes a student, who desires to secure a gun, to actually secure one.

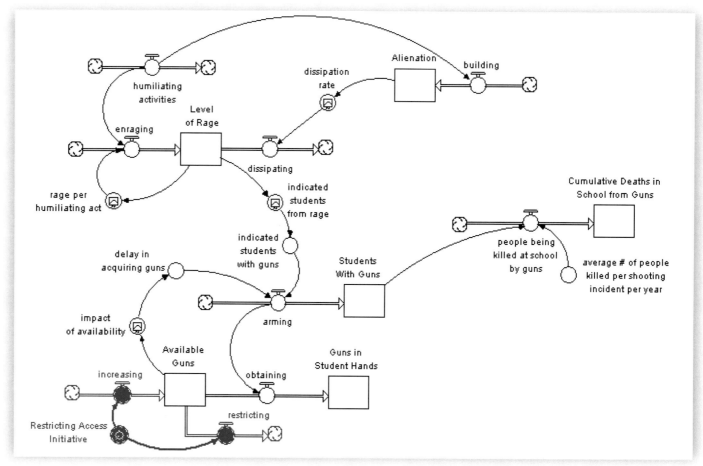

A value of 0 means the initiative is not in effect. A value of 100 means the initiative is 100% effective in restricting student access to available guns. This would mean new gun sales are completely cut off, and access to available guns is also cut off—though not instantly. Values between 0 and 100 have the corresponding intermediate impacts.

Restricting Access Initiative Results
A Policy Laboratory Dashboard

The Restricting Access Initiative is slightly more effective because it delays the occurrence of a shooting incident. The initiative is more proactive than the other two "gun-related" initiatives because it seeks to restrict student access to guns, rather than to detect and seize guns after students already have them. However, once again, this initiative does nothing to address the real reasons why students are looking for guns in the first place. As such, it cannot ultimately be effective in addressing the issue. However, used in combination with some other initiatives, it becomes an extra precaution—and, at least according to this model, one probably worth taking!

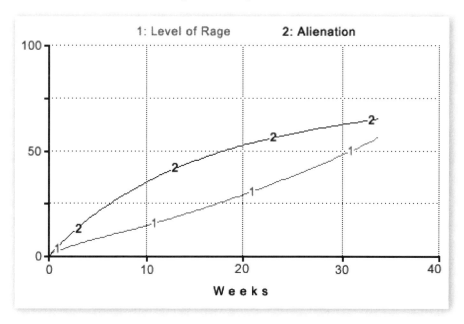

A Simulation-Generated Shooting Has Occurred!

Number of people killed in the incident   **5**

Week Number   **34**

Note: Your simulation results may differ due to a built-in variance for randomness.

Media Initiatives

4. Anti-Copycat Initiative

The Anti-Copycat Initiative is assumed to reduce the copycatting that is believed to occur as a result of the "head-lines" garnered by kids who commit violent acts with guns at school. The copycat effect is assumed to amplify the desire to seek vengeance by violent means when enraged.

It is assumed that the media (newspapers, TV, etc.) will continue to make school shootings front-page fare, and that continuing to do so will encourage "copycat" shootings. This initiative would reduce media coverage, or change it in a way that makes "copycat-ting" less likely.

A value of 0 means that initiative is not in effect. A value of 100 means the initiative that has been implemented is 100% effective – i.e., the copycat amplification effect is completely elimi-nated. This does not mean that school shoot-ings will cease! It means that any increase in shootings, due to media coverage, has been eliminated. Intermediate values between 0 and 100 have the correspon-ding intermediate impacts.

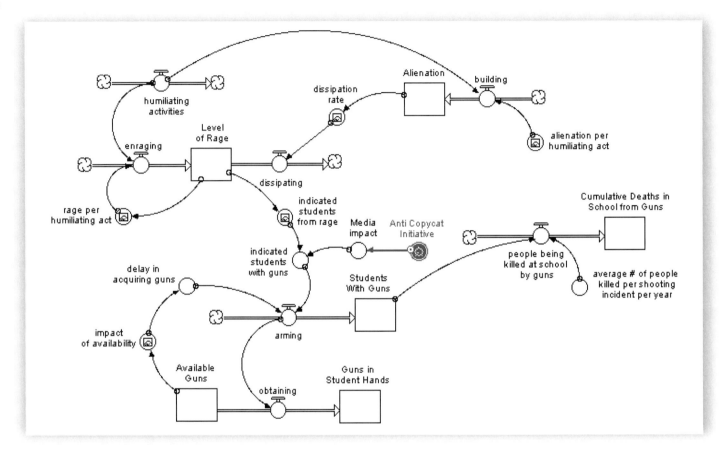

The Anti-Copycat Initiative, aside from probably being impossible to implement, is only modestly effective (at least in this model). The reason is that although media coverage may "glorify" shooting tragedies, and "give kids ideas," unless those kids are enraged, there's not much motive force to act in a violent manner. If they are enraged, the "headlines" may indeed provide further stimulation to express their feelings in a violent manner.

Anti-Copycat Initiative Results
A Policy Laboratory Dashboard

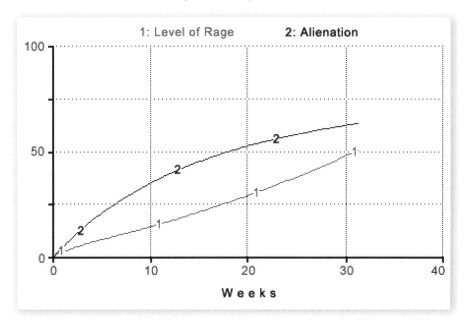

A Simulation-Generated Shooting Has Occurred!

Number of people killed in the incident   **5**

Week Number   **32**

Note: Your simulation results may differ due to a built-in variance for randomness.

Student Coping Skills Initiative

5. Rage Management Initiative

Rage Management is a two-pronged initiative. The first prong attacks the buildup of rage that comes from being the victim of humiliating acts. The initiative would target the building of coping skills that would enable a student to "process" the humiliating act in a way that did not lead to building up rage — or at least to building up less of it per humiliating act. In particular, efforts would be made to weaken the vicious cycle.

The second prong targets development of coping skills to prevent students from translating their rage — should it build up — into violent retribution with a gun. Measures would include making students acutely aware of the consequences of their actions — demystifying and un-glamorizing the associated violence.

A value of 0 means the initiative is not in place. A value of 100 means the initiative is 100% effective in attacking both the build-up of rage and the violent expression thereof. Intermediate values have the corresponding intermediate meanings.

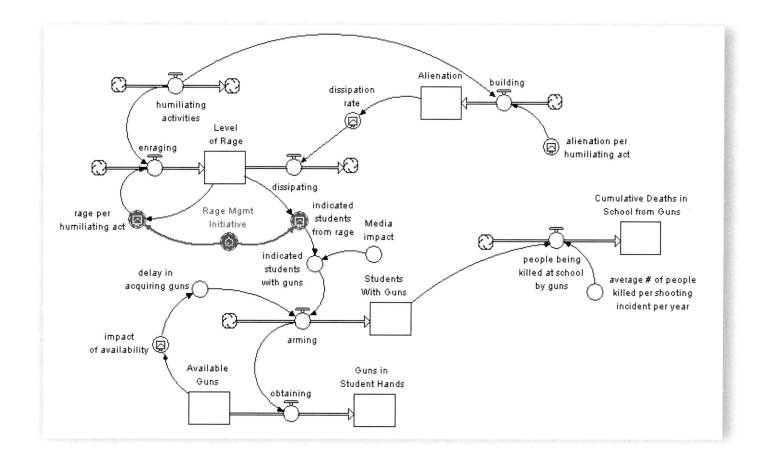

This is an interesting simulation! You heard no gunshots. However, as you can see from looking at the graph and numeric displays, levels of Rage and Alienation actually climbed above those recorded in simulations in which gunshots were heard. How come?

The answer lies in understanding the way the Rage Management Initiative impacts the system. Recall that the initiative is two-pronged — as is indicated in the detail of the portion of the model logic that is depicted on the next page.

Rage Management Initiative Results
A Policy Laboratory Dashboard

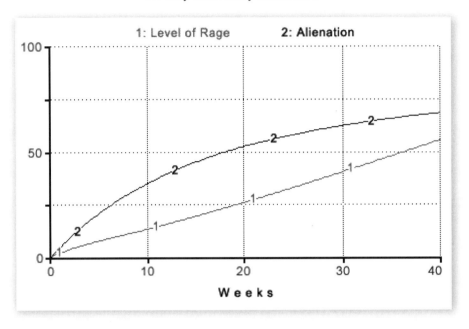

No Shooting Occurred!

Number of people killed   **0**
in the incident

Week Number   **40**

Note: Your simulation results may differ due to a built-in variance for randomness.

Rage Management Initiative Analysis

The initiative weakens the vicious cycle that drives the "enraging" inflow, but "humiliating activities" continue unabated, and the "Level of Rage" continues to build — albeit at a slower rate. The other prong of the initiative is targeted at the students expected to act on the feelings of rage via gun violence ("indicated students from rage"). Because the initiative is 100% effective, it essentially eliminates the "indicated students from rage." However, thwarting these actions does absolutely nothing to calm the rage! In fact, Alienation rises to a higher level, which means the dissipation of rage is depressed even more than in the Base Case. So the real question is...

If results like these were achieved in reality,

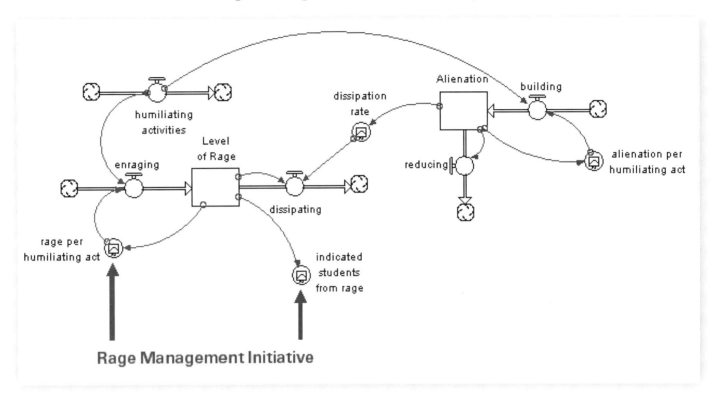

Rage Management Initiative

what would kids do with all the rage? It's highly unlikely it would go unexpressed. Hence, although no shooting incident occurs, the efficacy of this initiative, operating in isolation, should be considered "suspect."

Student Coping Skills Initiatives

6. Alienation Management Initiative

Alienation Management also is a two-pronged initiative. It is designed to reduce the sense of alienation that might otherwise build up as a result of being humiliated — or may have accumulated for other reasons.

The first prong targets development of coping skills for minimizing the amount of alienation that builds up per humiliating act that is endured. Measures include teaching students not to "withdraw" or "isolate themselves" if they have been the subject of humiliating actions, but rather to seek help from friends, guidance counselors, or other social contacts.

The second prong targets rapid reduction of any sense of alienation that might have built up. Here, again, measures would include teaching students to cope by sharing their feelings (as well as the incident) with counselors, friends and family — rather than bearing it all alone.

A value of 0 means that the initiative is not in place. A value of 100 means the initiative is 100% effective in eliminating both the build-up of alienation that comes from being subjected to humiliation, and in reducing any sense of alienation that may have accumulated.

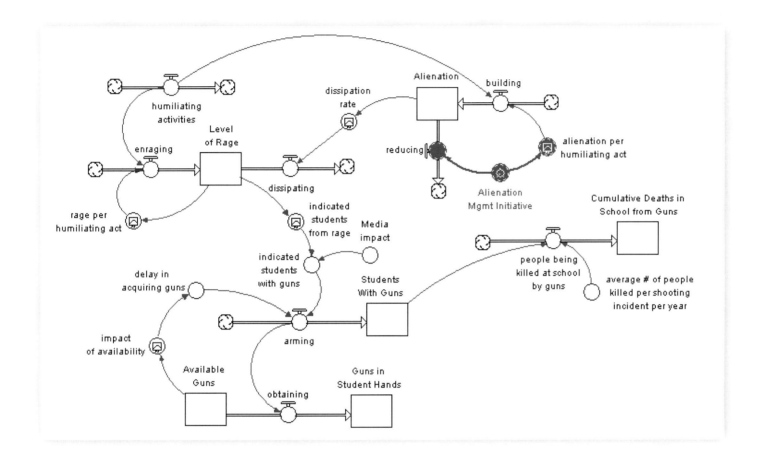

Another interesting simulation! This time, for the first time, we see both Rage and Alienation plateau-ing at lower levels. To understand what's going on, let's look at another detail of the portion of the logic showing how the Alienation Initiative works...

Alienation Management Initiative Results
A Policy Laboratory Dashboard

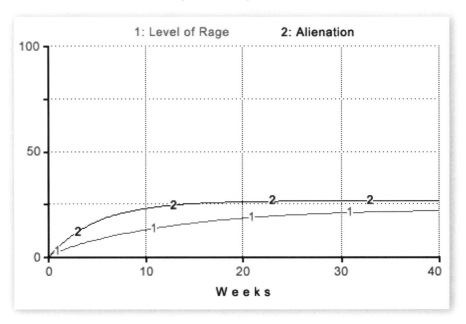

No Shooting Occurred!

Number of people killed   **0**
in the incident

Week Number   **40**

Note: Your simulation results may differ due to a built-in variance for randomness.

Alienation Management Initiative Analysis

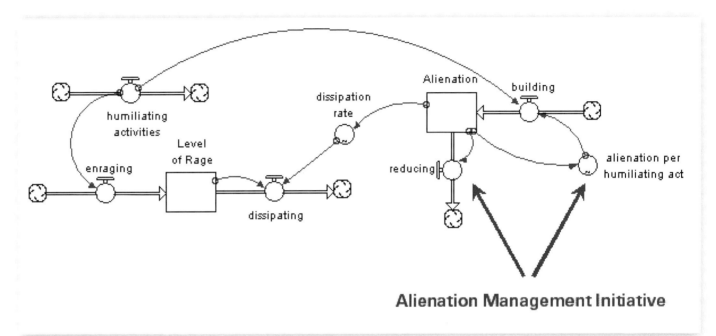

Alienation Management Initiative

The Alienation Management Initiative seeks to increase student coping skills that both mute the building-up of alienation that is driven by humiliating acts, and accelerate the reduction of alienation. The efficacy of this initiative depends on the validity of the assumptions that friends and other social contacts in a student's social network are an effective source of assistance with the dissipation of rage. By providing an outlet for expressing the feelings of a student who has been humiliated, the social network enables such students to effec- tively vent the rage that builds from having been subjected to humilia- tion. It appears that Alienation Management has the potential to be effective against rage- inspired violence.

Student Coping Skills Initiative

7. Humiliation Management Initiative

This initiative is aimed at reducing humiliating activities, in and outside of school.

It targets "humiliators" — the bullies and others who pick on, demean, make fun of, and otherwise belittle certain members of the student body. Measures could include an anonymous "hot line" that enables anyone to report humiliating acts they've observed, or experienced, to school officials.

A value of 0 means the initiative is not in place. A value of 100 (probably not achievable in reality), means 100% of such activities are eliminated. A value of 20 means a 20% reduction in these activities is achieved through implementation of the initiative.

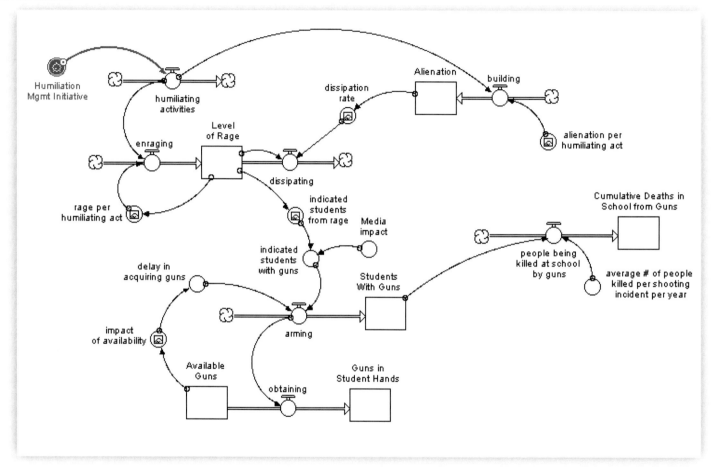

Humiliation Management Initiative Results
A Policy Laboratory Dashboard

The Humiliation Initiative, at 100%, completely eliminates all humiliating actions—something not achievable in practice. However as you'll discover in the "free form" section, even if only one-half of the humiliating activities are eliminated (with no other initiatives implemented!), neither rage nor alienation rise to levels significant enough to trigger violent activity.

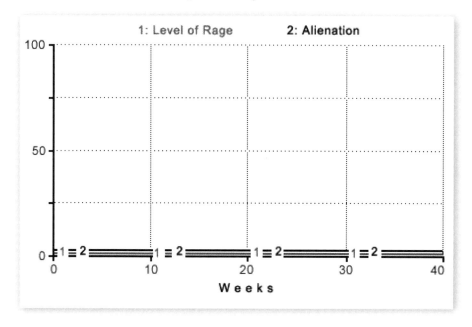

No Shooting Occurred!

Number of people killed in the incident   **0**

Week Number   **40**

Note: Your simulation results may differ due to a built-in variance for randomness.

Experiment Summary

Base Case – The base case shows the system with no initiatives in place.

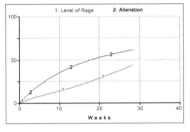

7 people killed
Week 28

Gun-Related Initiatives

1. Screening – The screening initiative aims to ensure that no guns enter the school through metal detection or searches.

Result at 100% – Screening does nothing to address built up rage. Shootings can still occur outside of school.

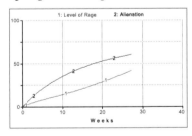

3 people killed
Week 26

2. Disarming – The disarming initiative takes guns out of the hands of students through intelligence programs to detect those with guns or access to guns.

Result at 100% – Disarming does nothing to address built up rage. It is nearly impossible to disarm enraged students who are very motivated to find and use guns.

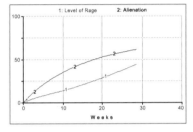

7 people killed
Week 28

3. Restricting Access – Restricting access attempts to reduce a student's ability to acquire a gun by penalizing parents or other adults that enable access or implementing tougher licensing laws.

Result at 100% – Restricting access does stifle a student's ability to acquire a gun but does not help release built up rage. It could be more effective when used in conjunction with coping skills.

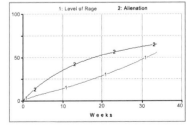

5 people killed
Week 34

Media Initiatives

4. Anti-Copycat – Reducing copycat behavior focuses on blocking or changing media coverage of in-school gun violence.

Result at 100% – The Anti-Copycat initiative is probably impossible to enforce and ineffective in that only enraged kids are encouraged by media coverage. Lacking rage, kids are not motivated to violence.

5 people killed
Week 32

Student Coping Skills Initiatives

5. Rage Management – Rage management training focuses on reducing the build-up of rage and steering feelings of rage away from violent expression.

Result at 100% – Rage management does reduce, or stop, gun violence in school. However, it does nothing to stop the humiliating events that continue to produce rage.

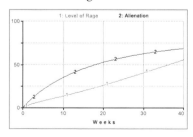

0 people killed
Week 40

6. Alienation Management – Alienation management teaches students to avoid isolation by seeking help from friends or trusted adults and reduce alienation by sharing feelings.

Result at 100% – This initiative is very effective at reducing school gun violence.

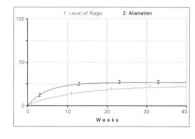

0 people killed
Week 40

7. Humiliation Management – Humiliation Management reduces humiliating events, in and outside of school.

Result at 100% – This initiative completely eliminates school gun violence. However, it is not realistic to assume that students will ever stop humiliating one another 100% of the time.

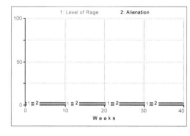

0 people killed
Week 40

The conclusion that emerges from this model is that if we want to stop gun-related violence (and presumably other types as well!) in our schools, we must target "humiliating activities" in all their forms. Measures could include programs to raise consciousness in the student body with respect to the dynamics that are set in motion by such activities, and also the associated consequences of engaging in these activities. Those consequences probably should be quite harsh (like immediate expulsion). Other measures could include setting up an anonymous "hot line" for students to report any humiliating activities they perceive. Only by cracking down hard on humiliators, and creating a school culture that does not support or tolerate humiliation, will it be possible to cut off the source of the killings and other violence that results from the associated build-up of rage. Combined with other initiatives—particularly rage and alienation management initiatives—a Humiliation Management initiative would be even more effective!

CHAPTER 5

Searching for High-Leverage Points

As we learned in Chapter 4, system behavior can be difficult to change. It seemed a good bet that disarming students or installing metal detectors to screen for weapons would have stopped gun violence in schools. Perhaps you were surprised when shots were still fired — outside the school building.

When Systems Thinkers try to understand a problem and its potential solutions, they look for "high leverage points." Leverage points are changes in the model that result in a shift in behavior. High leverage points are model entities whose values, when altered only a small amount, result in a shift in behavior.

In this chapter, you will have the opportunity to look for high leverage points through free-form experimentation with the model. You can combine various policy initiatives set at any level of implementation (from 0 to 100%) and also vary many of the model's behavioral assumptions. Ideally, you are looking for a mix of initiatives that is effective in reducing gun-related violence under a wide range of behavioral assumptions.

Before we begin free-form experimentation, let's review the model's behavioral assumptions. There are five behavorial assumptions that fall into two categories:

Psychology-related
1. Indicated Students from Rage
2. Rage per Humiliating Act
3. Dissipation Rate
4. Alienation per Humiliating Act

Gun-related
5. Impact of Availability

Each behavioral assumption is represented by a special graph called a graphical function.

Graphical functions show the relationships between variables in the model. When one model variable changes, the other will change depending on the author's perception and understanding of what happens in reality. These behavioral assumptions are often referred to by Systems Thinkers as "mental models."

Psychology-related Behavioral Assumptions

1. Indicated Students from Rage

This graph represents the author's assumption of what the relationship is between level of rage and the number of students who arm themselves.

Level of Rage has an arbitrary range of 0 to 100. The values are relative, meaning 0 is no rage and 100 is the maximum rage one can feel. Notice that students do not desire to arm themselves for purposes of expressing their rage until rage climbs above 30% of the maximum rage they could possibly feel. After this threshold is crossed, an increasing number of students feel driven to seek violent retribution. The curve is very steep between rage levels of 30 and 70.

To summarize this behavorial assumption, low levels of rage have little impact on the number of students who arm themselves. However, once a certain threshold has been reached (say 30%), small changes in the level of rage have large consequences (up until a certain point.)

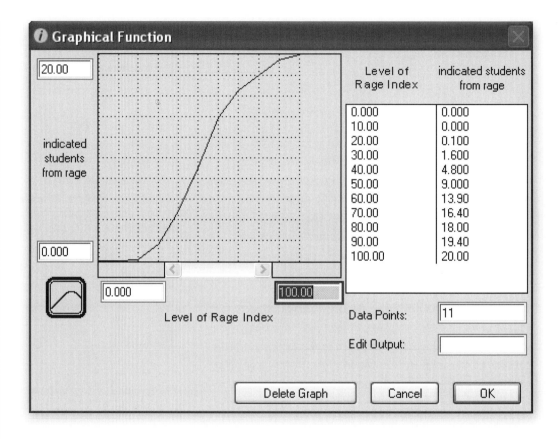

Level of Rage Index	indicated students from rage
0.000	0.000
10.00	0.000
20.00	0.100
30.00	1.600
40.00	4.800
50.00	9.000
60.00	13.90
70.00	16.40
80.00	18.00
90.00	19.40
100.00	20.00

Data Points: 11

Edit Output:

Psychology-related Behavioral Assumptions

2. Rage per Humiliating Act

This graph represents the rather straightforward relationship between level of rage and rage per humiliating act. As the level of rage increases, the rage per humiliating act also increases.

The more rage a student is already feeling, the more rage they will build up from any act of humiliation they endure. That is, if a student is already "simmering," even a small humiliating act can add a substantial amount to the level of rage they are feeling. This relationship helps to create a vicious cycle.

Note that there is a sharper effect at higher levels of rage. That steepness pushes the vicious cycle even more.

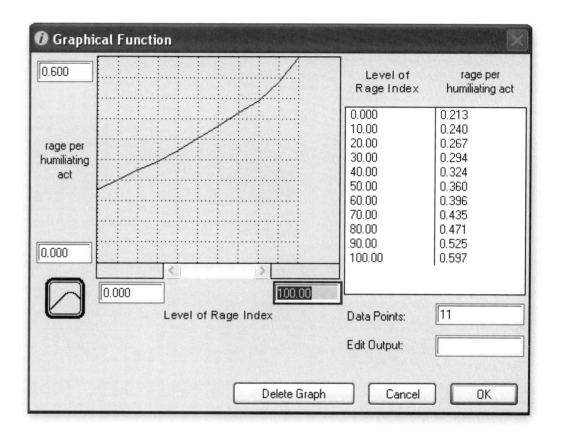

Level of Rage Index	rage per humiliating act
0.000	0.213
10.00	0.240
20.00	0.267
30.00	0.294
40.00	0.324
50.00	0.360
60.00	0.396
70.00	0.435
80.00	0.471
90.00	0.525
100.00	0.597

Psychology-related Behavioral Assumptions

3. Dissipation Rate

Alienation and the dissipation of rage have an inverse relationship.

The higher the level of alienation the student feels, the more slowly they will dissipate their feelings of rage. Friends, and other social contacts, are assumed to play a vital role in helping students to effectively and expeditiously "process" their rage in the event that it has built up.

When alienation is low, the dissipation of rage is high. The curve is the steepest when alienation goes from 0 to 10. So as alienation moves from 0 to 10, the dissipation of rage decreases more rapidly than at any other amount of alienation. The author is making the assumption that the dissipation of rage is more sensitive to the level of alienation when it is at the lower end of the scale. As the level of alienation moves toward 50 and above, the dissipation rate slows down and does not change as significantly as it did for the lower levels of alienation.

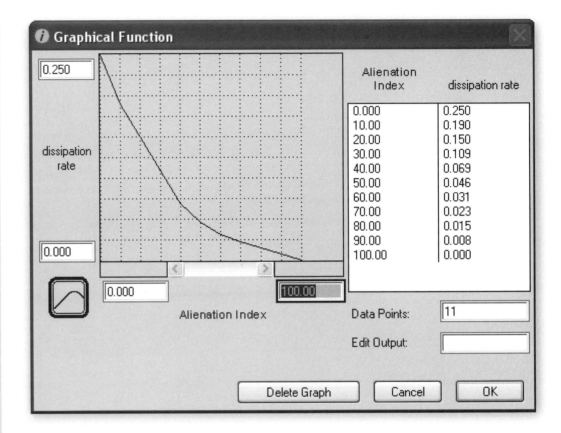

Alienation Index	dissipation rate
0.000	0.250
10.00	0.190
20.00	0.150
30.00	0.109
40.00	0.069
50.00	0.046
60.00	0.031
70.00	0.023
80.00	0.015
90.00	0.008
100.00	0.000

Psychology-related Behavioral Assumptions

4. Alienation per Humiliating Act

As the level of alienation a student feels increases, the amount of alienation that is generated per humiliating act increases. Another vicious cycle! Essentially, it's saying that when a kid feels isolated and alone, even small acts of humiliation (or perceived humiliation) contribute to furthering the overall sense of alienation.

Notice that when there is no alienation (0) and a humiliating act occurs, the amount of alienation that is generated per act is .5. As alienation increases, the amount of alienation generated per act increases more with each new act.

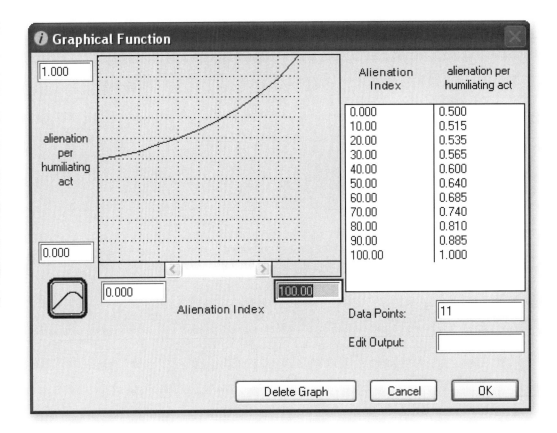

Alienation Index	alienation per humiliating act
0.000	0.500
10.00	0.515
20.00	0.535
30.00	0.565
40.00	0.600
50.00	0.640
60.00	0.685
70.00	0.740
80.00	0.810
90.00	0.885
100.00	1.000

Gun-related Behavioral Assumptions

5. Impact of Availability

Even if students want to give voice to their rage by seeking retribution with guns, the lack of access to firearms can stymie those desires. The model assumes that the availability of guns influences how long it takes for students to acquire a gun if they are seeking to do that. The higher the number of available guns, the shorter the delay is in obtaining them.

When the available guns index is low, the impact of availability is high, meaning there is a long delay to getting a gun. This is another inverse relationship. The curve is the steepest between 0 and 0.2, meaning the longest delay occurs when guns first become available.

To summarize this behaviorial assumption, the author believes that having a smaller number of available guns than normal (less than 1.0 index) would lead to much longer delays in obtaining guns. Likewise, once there are more guns available than normal, having a lot more guns would have little effect.

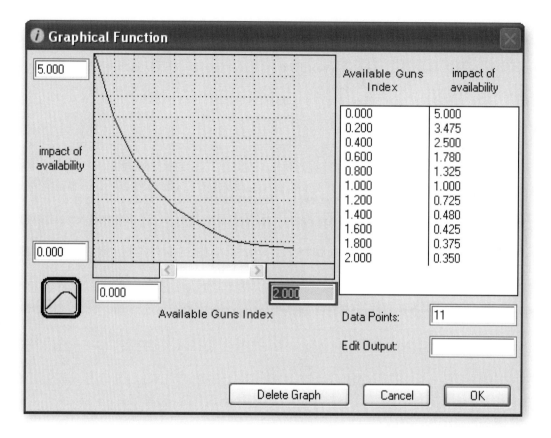

Available Guns Index	impact of availability
0.000	5.000
0.200	3.475
0.400	2.500
0.600	1.780
0.800	1.325
1.000	1.000
1.200	0.725
1.400	0.480
1.600	0.425
1.800	0.375
2.000	0.350

Getting Started

In order to find those policy initiatives with the most impact on reducing gun-related violence, you need to identify your assumptions about system behavior and then test them in a simulation context. On the *Policy Initiatives* screen, you're able to manipulate the level of implementation for each policy initiative. On the *Assumptions* screen, you can see and change behavorial assumptions about gun-related violence in schools.

Once you've set initiative implementation levels and your behavioral assumptions, you'll use Dashboard II to see their impact on the system and gun-related violence. Dashboard II will show the levels of rage and alienation that result from your assumption and initiative changes.

To move between the screens and test your initiative choices and assumptions:

1. Click on *Searching for High Leverage Points* from the Main Menu

2. On Dashboard II, click on *To Initiatives*.

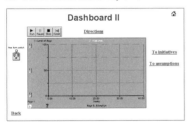

3. To change initiative implementation levels, move the knob. Note the knob has a number of other options available:

• For a reminder of the initiative definition, click on the ? button.

• To undo your implementation settings, click on the U button on the knob.

• To review how an initiative is implemented in the model, click the name of the initiative.

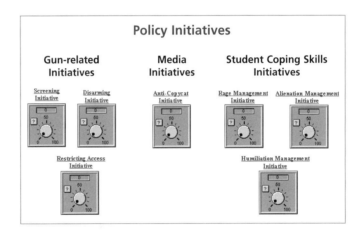

4. Click *Back* to return to *Dashboard II*.

5. To see and change assumptions, click on *To Assumptions*.

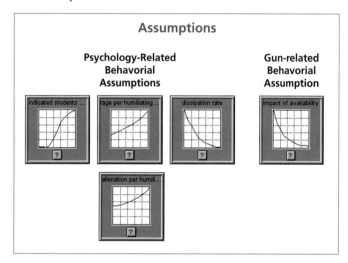

6. To change an assumption, double-click on the graph, You can sketch a new graph by dragging your mouse pointer along the grid or editing the numeric values. To edit a numeric value, click on it and enter the new value in the Edit Output box. After exiting the graph, you can click the *U* icon that will appear to restore the assumption to its default curve.

7. Click *Back* to return to *Dashboard II* and test your initiatives and assumptions.

8. Turn on the *free form switch* by clicking on it.

Free Form Switch

9. Click the *Run* button.

As you experiment, compare your assumptions and results about gun violence in schools with the default assumptions and their results. It's in the comparing that you'll begin to learn about guns at school, understand what leads to violence and what can be done to reduce school killings. Of course, you'll learn even more as you discuss your findings with others.

A Quick Example

The assumptions review and Getting Started instructions have equipped you to experiment at will in your search for high leverage points. If you want, read and follow along with this example to get an even better idea of how initiative implementation levels and assumptions work together to change system behavior and impact gun violence in our modeled school.

First we'll set some initiative implementation levels.

1. Go to the *Policy Initiatives* screen.

Remember that the screening initiative that places metal detectors and other monitoring equipment at school entrances and includes activities like locker searches was not effective in eliminating school gun violence even when set at 100%. On the other hand, there's no reason to allow guns in school. In fact, some amount of screening sends an important message that the school cares about safety.

2. Set the *Screening Initiative* to 50.

In Chapter 4 we learned that Humiliation and Alienation Management were both very effective in reducing gun violence when set at 100%. But, it is impractical, not to mention impossible, to manage away all humiliation and alienation. You may do a great job with the current student body only to have an already enraged student move into the school from another district. It does, however, seem to be wise to manage levels of humiliation and rage.

3. Set both the *Alienation Management Initiative* and the *Humiliation Management Initiative* to 80.

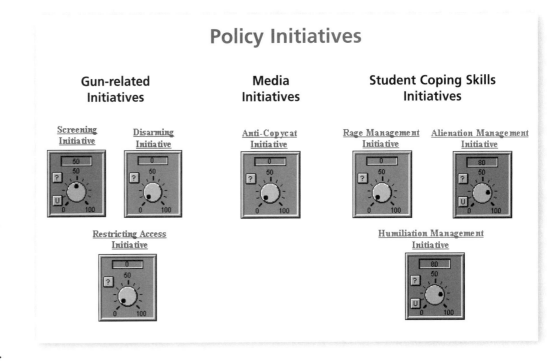

This is how the new settings should look.

Now we need to set the model's behavorial assumptions.

1. Click on *Back* to return to *Dashboard II* and then click on *To Assumptions*.

Since the relationship between humiliation, alienation and rage is so critical, let's focus on the assumption about Alienation per Humiliating Act.

2. Double-click on the *Alienation per Humiliating Act* graph.

The model's author assumes that when there is no alienation and a humiliating act occurs, the amount of alienation that is generated per act is 0.5. As alienation increases, the amount of alienation generated per act of humiliation increases.

We agree that alienation and humiliation are a vicious cycle; as a student becomes more humiliated, her alienation grows and as alienation grows her ability to dissipate the rage associated with humiliation grows. But let's say that we don't think that alienation builds so quickly. The vast majority of students have some way to deal with humiliation — friends, family, teachers, activities — so we'll change the assumption about how quickly alienation grows with each humiliating act.

3. Draw a new graph that starts at 0.3 on the y-axis, then very slowly builds up to 0.85.

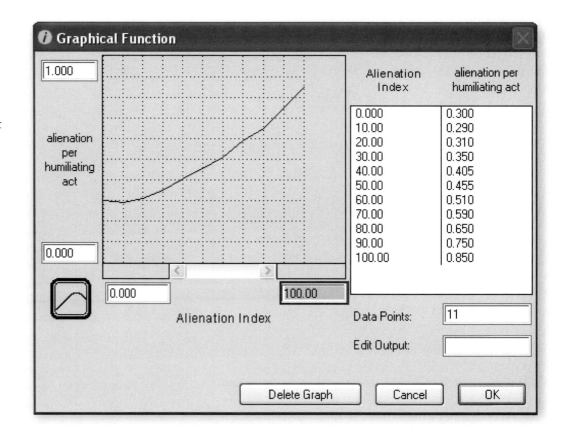

Alienation Index	alienation per humiliating act
0.000	0.300
10.00	0.290
20.00	0.310
30.00	0.350
40.00	0.405
50.00	0.455
60.00	0.510
70.00	0.590
80.00	0.650
90.00	0.750
100.00	0.850

Free Form Results

Dashboard II

Let's test our settings and new assumption.

1. Click on _Back_ to return to _Dashboard II_.

2. Turn on the _free form switch_ by clicking on it.

3. Click on the _Run_ button.

We've really reduced gun violence in our modeled school through high leverage point initiatives!

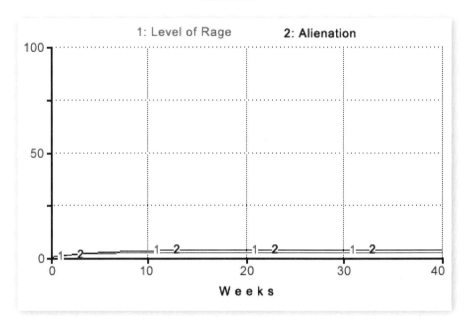

No Shooting Occurred!

Number of people killed in the incident   **0**

Week Number   **40**

CHAPTER 6
Summary

Barry Richmond's original intent for his Story of the Month series was to stimulate discussion and provide clarity to complicated social issues. Like so many social problems, the factors related to gun violence in schools are hard to predict and control using traditional methods of thinking. Systems Thinking gives us a disciplined way to think through the dynamic relationships between causes and outcomes, including both the physical and psychological factors. By providing a common language and a framework for visualizing problems, Systems Thinking allows people from any discipline to develop a shared understanding and work together towards the best possible solution. Doctors, social workers, teachers, law enforcement officials, politicians can all apply their educations, experiences, and view points using the same set of constructs.

Today, Systems Thinking is being widely applied in academic settings – from high school science classes to graduate school research projects – as well as professional settings including health care, manufacturing, finance, government, defense, and research and development. In many instances, Systems Thinkers are being helped by software applications such as STELLA and *iThink* from isee systems.

isee systems (formerly High Performance Systems) is the world leader and innovator in Systems Thinking software. Founded in 1985, isee released STELLA®, the first software application to bring Systems Thinking to the desktop. In addition to STELLA, which is primarily used by educators, isee offers *iThink*® for business simulation.

In addition to developing software, isee systems continues the mission of its founder, Barry Richmond, by offering training programs in Systems Thinking application. Books like this one and others that introduce readers to Systems Thinking and how to use it in classroom and business settings are also published by isee systems.

For more information about Systems Thinking, we suggest these resources:

isee systems, inc	www.iseesystems.com
Creative Learning Exchange	www.clexchange.org
Pegasus Communications	www.pegasuscom.com
Society for Organizational Learning	www.solonline.org
Sustainability Institute	www.sustainabilityinstitute.org
System Dynamics Society	www.systemdynamics.org
Systems Thinking in Schools	www.watersfoundation.org

Acknowledgments

Special thanks to Steve Peterson and Karim Chichakly for their help and guidance adapting this *Story of Month* and sharing the insights of true Systems Thinkers.

www.iseesystems.com

Phone 603 448 4990   Fax 603 448 4992

Technical Support: support@iseesystems.com